the tossing dream

poems by

jade rosina mccutcheon

Finishing Line Press
Georgetown, Kentucky

the tossing dream

Copyright © 2023 by jade rosina mccutcheon
ISBN 979-8-88838-227-1 First Edition
All rights reserved under International and Pan-American Copyright Conventions. No part of this book may be reproduced in any manner whatsoever without written permission from the publisher, except in the case of brief quotations embodied in critical articles and reviews.

ACKNOWLEDGMENTS

This collection of poetry owes a great deal of gratitude to the Oregon poetry societies and groups I have been fortunate to be involved with. Poetry might manifest on the lonely rock out at sea but the work of believing in it and allowing it to move into print can only happen with the support and belief of one's fellow poets. I thank the Salem Poetry Project, Mid-Valley Poetry Society, Head for the Hills, Silverton Poetry Association, and the Oregon Poetry Association for the many wonderful opportunities they have offered me in my growth as a poet. A huge thank you to Janice Cipriani-Willis and Dorland Mountain Arts where two artist residencies in 2021 and 2022 allowed me the space and landscape to put together this chapbook.

I would like to thank Eleanor Berry, my brother Bruce, Berri, Brian, Henry and Eleanor Leslie for their loving support and my dear friends across the globe in Salem, Dallas (OR), Davis (CA), Los Angeles, San Francisco, London, Sydney, Bathurst, Glenlyon, Daylesford, Melbourne, Adelaide, Bolwarra and Hill End. We are all connected, this writing is the kaleidoscopic lens formed at the places where we meet.

Publisher: Leah Huete de Maines
Editor: Christen Kincaid
Cover Art: Jade Rosina McCutcheon
Author Photo: Jade Rosina McCutcheon
Cover Design: Elizabeth Maines McCleavy

Order online: www.finishinglinepress.com
also available on amazon.com

Author inquiries and mail orders:
Finishing Line Press
PO Box 1626
Georgetown, Kentucky 40324
USA

Table of Contents

Winter 1
Passing 2
The Garden 3
A Humming 4
The Poet 5
Close 6
The Lake 7
Popcorn 8
On the Coast 9
Invisible in Fall 10
Listen 11
Late Night Call 12
The Tossing Dream 13
2020 14
Fire 15
Wake 16
Sitting 18
Pandemic 19
The Veil 20
One Thing 21
In the Dog Park All Things Are Equal 22
Fishing 23
Brother 25
Aussie Rusty Rain Tank 26
Alice Springs 27
Parched 28
The Singer 29
Two Poets in the Park 30
One Gold Tear 32
Woman 33
Meditation 34

Winter

The leaves are fallen
rust red golden
back to mother earth
deeply private blues

feather fluttering flock
perching precociously
promenading for position
on the seed block,
source of life
just outside
my mother's window.

Her frail lilac face
watches these winged harlequins
sky dancers
vibrant against grey.

No need to grab the walker
or to rug up
for a treacherous marathon outside
into the land of hidden traps.

She can just sit
and dream
dry old lips
softly sipping tea

treasuring her final
season of cold
magic blue rose red
into Winter.

Passing

A moment of
 daphne hangs
in the air
        stopping me

in the perfumed space
    between now and
memory
        hanging like

a sweet kiss
        suspended on
moonlight thread

as though you were
            dropping in
to remind me
that your sweet soul

lives on.

The Garden

Pollen dancers
escort flowering
seeds of memory
      oh the flutter
of shadows wingspanned
creaking gate in the wind.

Monet's perfect path
lace violet turquoise blue iris
rose pink peony against
sunburst red amaryllis.

One hundred dead wishes
stir on the ground
blood red leaves are stirring
a heavenly, deadly sound.

I fall deeply
another room
      off the path
hollow filled
with past dreams.

How soft, how sweet
      Georgia O'Keefe knew how to paint
      a skeleton
           white against blue
                body's poetry of death waiting,
      disintegrating, etched.

I have arrived at sunset
perfectly lost in lilac.

A Humming

Sinking deeper
the rusty bell tolls
gray fox dances

Scorpio full moon
sidles over the ridge
whirring hummingbird hovers.

Rose pink vista
evening sky
held fast by gold.

Hummingbird dances
for me in front of
world-tired eyes

'don't give up, there's so much more
to be done.'

The Poet

She lives in an old
run down hut
by the sea
in solitude.

A cup of tea
sound of gulls
waves breaking
pen in hand

sculpting words
castles in the sand.

Her notebooks
cover shores
where imprisoned words
scream at her
demanding to be
scavenged into

verse scattered
amongst the waves
hidden in rock pools
lost in hermit shells

dreaming of an ancient treasure seeker
old soul-smith who by moonlight
arranges them
sets them free.

Close

You wake me
from the last dream
into this blue ache breeze

owl holy hoots
vibrate me to soft spaces
under flowering gums
at night with you

breath meets breath

reaching
        soft skin
                close to clear
                        rushing stream

deer nuzzles earth
by my cheek
stars fall across
vision.

The Lake

I am walking my memory path
perfect circle energy labyrinth
enfolding deep lake water
tracing moments of blue unbearable

I remember the song of the path
with every crunching step.

Here, I prayed and wept deep amber
there, I laughed ecstatic with heart swell joy.

One magical easter evening
silver moonlight sliver revealed
the sword of the lady of the lake to me
just out of reach.

I remember how I ached soft rose to try
to touch the sacred.

On that curve my perfect dog would dive
into deep cool, more bliss than should be allowed.

By those reeds I made peace with my soul
in the still, obsidian night.

I once ran screaming family blood wounds
three times past the moon's broken reflection
until finally

I became the water
the tree
the be-ing

vibrating invisible sound
like an earthwise gong.

Popcorn

I struggle with
my popcorn mind
as I try to write

treading water in a deep sea
floating, sinking, swimming words
offering endless
naval vessel designs.

You just lie there
across my path
gopher snake extraordinaire
perfect in your own design

diamond eyes
noting my imperfect
nature.

You somehow know it is my lot
to eternally toil with words
disguised as pigeons, crows,
clouds, death, heaven

and yes, maybe even you
my nature perfect friend.

I'm assuming you wouldn't
be interested in some popcorn?

On the Coast

Grains of sand
seapspray mind
seeking silence
as I count them
                one, two, three

ballerina seagulls soar
my mind sets off
                across this vast ocean

a space later

I look at my hand
still holding
earth's history

glinting as it falls
through my fingers

I have forgotten
what I'm doing
it's as though

I was
                in the middle
                              of something.

Invisible in Fall

Walking again always
eternally forever
footstep after footstep
occasionally losing balance
on the acorns, steep hills
carpets of wet Fall leaves

that sort of thing
mostly just
walking the path softly.

Today a chance blue-golden meeting between the trees.

Dakota woman walking
tells me the Indian school
founded in 1880
was firing the indigenous teachers
replacing them
with white teachers.

She had had taught for 39 years
with a master's degree and a PhD
in Native American literature.

Maybe it was the sudden gust of wind
or too many acorns

my balance was lost.

Denial of an entire people's voice

 the crushing of that voice.

High is the cost of assimilation
for those whose culture has been taken
from them.

Quite a fall from our cultural path.

Listen

Cassandra's violet voice
could not stop
slipping sliding
fault lines.

We are at
the vulnerable
edge
truth unheard

all still
before the cracking

here it comes.

Like a soft drop
on the mind
like a red leaf drifting
across an open sea

from long forgotten spaces
of ignorance and greed

       surprise!

Niagara falling,
icicles, world markets,
only the first crack

       shhhh it comes.

Late Night Call

You scream maniacally
outside my bedroom window
it's 3am
sleep shattered shuttered.

Horror movie
soundtrack
a woman dying
think Psycho.

Vermillion death tongue
rips me from my dreams
visions of hell
raw flesh.

So close
breath in my room
I am alive
still at least.

You screaming red fox
I needed therapy
after your visit
(touched as I was).

Did you sign up
for that piercing scream
or was it just
the luck of the draw?

Don't tell me
it's your courting voice
I will surely
die laughing.

The Tossing Dream

The river rises
again tonight
swirling swelling silently
dreams across the tossing
landscape.

Silver full moon
light floods
reflections hiding
delicate disasters
underwater sleek sediments
mired in soggy social media
'it's a swell life' and drugs.

A fierce fire too close
bags packed toothbrush
on the top
burning flesh blind
mind searing wind erasure
we watch the television
glued like moths.

In my dream I drown,
am blown away
burnt like a chicken
split apart
total upheaval
mother earth has put me
on notice.

2020

Dropping hard
dressed sponge soft
onto an already beaten road
2020 fell
like a mammoth
from a forgotten
karmic star
right on top of our
pre-occupied heads.

It was as though
the sidewalk
cracked apart
while we were out
walking
looking at the birds
watching the leaves fall
buying new cars

then there was nothing there
just an infinite
deep-dark space
with Cassandra's soft haunting song
in the distance.

Twenty-twenty
often
used to describe
perfect vision
to look ahead

understand what's coming.

Fire

I rest between two worlds
between earth and sky
between one country and another
between one god and another.

I hear the land speak across
this divide
I hear the gods speak
in all languages.

I rest between two worlds
between my breath and your breath
between my leader and your leader
between my life and your death.

I breathe with the oak
between roots and leaves
you breathe in the smoke
the ashes leave.

I am connected to you
and you are burning
I cannot rest
this is you and me.

Wake

Does it ache already
blood on snow
shooting through sleet
crusted sermons
jabbing your thoughts
with pinprick precision.

Did the fires
remind you
did the death of your grandma
remind you
does the threat of war
remind you.

We do not
have long
on this earth
and we die
every moment
of every day.

A koala dead
a national monument
destroyed
a black woman shot
a young boy
drowned
a boat capsizing
lost dark water
you are hurting.

What are you
doing here
this day
this life
this earth
where is your
mind
what do you
want
how will you
speak?

Sitting

I find myself
here
in the deep red sunlight
of a fading world

praying to
our dying earth
while distant sounds
of cracking glaciers
of war
cruelty and abuse
guns and bombs
trigger me

they are more final

not about who
will win
but who
will be left
on earth
to watch
the setting
sun.

Pandemic

My mask
my hands
going out
the cart
the card
my hands
my gloves
the door
did I touch   did I touch
my hands
my gloves
my clothes
my face
death   in the air.

I try not   to breathe.

The Veil.
> *'All the news just repeats itself like some forgotten dream.'* John Prine.

I dreamt you were with me when it happened
we were running to the center of the field
with thousands of other souls
towards a huge beam of light
it was as though we all knew this was it
I held out my hand and you took it.

I woke up to the sound of a vacuum cleaner
a hungry sucking sound gnawing on my brain
the colors in the room were different
intense, loud, overwhelming radiating red, blue and yellow.

You called and asked if I'd like to meet for coffee
like nothing had happened
as though our world hadn't ended
as though you weren't in my dream running beside me
the one person in my life who knew what I knew
wired the same way
'meet for coffee?'

I was in a dark room with the television on
I had seen this news before
disaster after disaster all around the world
between the earthquakes and hurricanes
were all the advertisements for drugs
you can take to pretend this isn't happening
for every ache and pain, every limp and wobble
there was a drug that had been tested and declared 'safe'
by some anacronym hiding between the networks.

Am I dead, did the apocalypse happen
this dream, this memory of the 'news 'plays
over and over when the memory of the end only appears
in something called a dream that my friend
doesn't remember and no-one ever mentions.

One Thing

Sometimes there's
nothing left
to do

except to make
your coffee

if that's all
there is left
to do
why not
make it
perfect coffee?

Fair trade
organic rich dark nutty beans
grind them
finely
sweetly
kindly.

Use the special
expresso machine
you bought yourself
way back when

sit back
gaze out
at the old oak
sigh and breathe
inhale

the aroma

the one thing
that came to you
to do on this perfect day.

In the Dog Park All Things Are Equal

In the dog park
we don't care
if the dog owner is a republican
or democratic
atheist or born again
old or young
Indian or Australian
from New York or Idaho,
we don't care
because it just
isn't relevant.

Dog owners only
want to know
'do our dogs get along'?

The entire transaction
is built around that one question
everything else floats
mindlessly
over the breezy treetops.

If they do get along
hallelujah and praise the doggy gods
we can talk for hours
about anything
but if our mutts
decide they aren't kin
then the passing will be brief.

'Have a nice day'
sidles over the interaction
like a warm milk balm
and owners move on
with the love of their life
agreeing that the other dog
wasn't up to snuff
or sniff
for that matter.

Fishing

It was the simplest
of adventures
a brown paper bag
with sandwiches
a bottle of milk
fishing gear consisting of line
wrapped around cork.

6 am three kids
into the old green chevvy
and off we'd go.

He was a big man
green shorts
checkered shirt
no hat or sunscreen
he loved to fish
loved to be
on the water
in a rowboat
just floating
quiet.

It was never about
the fishing
although lines
were thrown
sandwiches eaten
milk drunk
it was the relief from discord
the memory of war.

The peace
in that little
rundown rowboat
was more than heaven
it was acceptance

that my dad
and us kids
accepted each other

waiting for fish to bite
was a sideline business.

Brother

I am thinking of you
dark blue green
knowing you
silent scream
trapped and staring
hungry as a child
earth weary old man
silver bright mind
on old giraffe knees.

If we'd known then
as we played
in our childhood
hornets' nest
choices would become
habits
locking us onto
untenable life paths

        what world minstrels
        we might have become.

Here we are
worlds apart
hands reaching
for each other's heart
worn and torn
from this dark life
knowing too well
the deep ruts
and ditches
that led us
to this
age.

Be light
upon yourself
be light
unto yourself.

Aussie Rusty Rain Tank

In times of deep change
a world pandemic
for example,
new ways must be
found for
old problems.

As I sit in rainy Oregon
gazing into charcoal night
contemplating loyal Venus
chasing her rascal silver moon
around and around the earth,
my dear Australian friends
are rolling a rusty old water tank
down a dusty dry road.

They ask the brawny
local handyman to turn on
his golden blue torch
and cut the tank in half,
 two full moons
where they could store
their wood for winter.

Just a little muscle power
with lightbulb ingenuity
a dash of good deeds
un soupçon of 'making do'
mixed with a good laugh
a 'goodonya matey
want a beer?'

Sometimes
we need to break our orbit
round about our earth
re-invent ourselves

like an Aussie rusty rain tank
that just needed
rolling down the road.

Alice Springs

Scarlet dusty mandarin
sun explodes on my left
silver purple sickle moon
rises to the heavens on my right
as I enter Alice.

Rough as guts red earth road cuts
through deep blue midnight
dragging orange dirt-cloud red
yesterdays with it
days that are tired like
holy socks.

This dusty track across
carved moonscape desert
draws me into the old one's heart
lying dormant deep below
ancient protector, Uluru.

Like Alice I fall downwards
landing in eternity between
deep wise roots and ancestors.

I slumber beneath the dream
a long time
lost in an equation
just noticing
I am here.

The movement from one world
to the next
is deceptively small

and still.

Parched

She walks across the desert
carrying an urn full of water
the only water for miles.

She knows it's value
when everyone around
has none.

A little like love.

The water carrier stops
places the urn on the sand
no-one comes near.

The water might be poisoned
the water might have conditions
the water is not to be trusted.

The urn is still there
in the endless sand
and she

she has long since gone.

The Singer

She plays her harp
peace white pond
lily tunes
crystal silver voice
canary golden breath
floating in peacock blue air.

Long-armed diggers
in the pub halt
their swig halfway
to ever-open mouths

all the inhabitants
of this sunset
end of the road
Eden once gold land

pause

arrested by her voice
shattering amber light
across windowpanes.

Two Poets in the Park

A Mondrian cubist yellow butterfly
dances past two Andy Warhol poets
soft light hair framed
hard against peacock sky.

We share haiku
enquire about grandchildren
the Portland protests
fires and covid.

Spring flowers spin
        da Vinci swirl
for a moment
as blue jays screech
mocking Monet
with their dazzling cobalt garb.

A ride-on mower
chews through the moment
cubing space and time
the poets nod and laugh

dropping words like petals.

One Gold Tear

Seven empty rooms containing
seven wefty looms thunder grey and cloud soaked
from the bottom of their wombs
'let us go' the looms did cry
into the dripping air
'the seven maids have long since gone
these rooms have fallen bare'.

A passing crow heard their plea
and wept one gold tear mid-flight
it spun and wove a spinning top
smashing a window bringing light.

The golden teardrop filled the rooms
like a brilliant fiery balm
one loom was spinning, another singing
another telling a yarn.

The crow brought friends and peacock plumes
laughing, bringing gifts
a sad old loom kicked off her shoes
danced quicksteps on wooden feet.

All it took was one gold tear
one compassionate note
for the empty looms to start spinning their tunes
weaving rugs and fine gold coats.

The seven looms now in golden rooms
weave garments in gorgeous cloth
grateful for the gift of one kind crow
just listening was all it cost.

Woman

She sits and stares
out to infinite sunset
listening to the song
of light on her path.

She pushes her world
through universal streets
in eternal storms
down rabbit holes
into looking glass.

She stands
on the edge of a cliff
buffeting overload
she is brave.

She hides quietly
in the darkness downstairs
hoping he will never find her

he who needs her pain.

She runs her business
endlessly inside the swamp
while raising her kids
in a colour-blind state.

She is tired of being quiet
tired of waiting for the moon
aching for her earth-wise knowledge
to be heard.

    A soft clicking
    the key turns
    her voice finally
    unlocks her world.

Meditation

Will I stumble awake
before I leave
recognize the moment
here

take my life
in my hands
walk through
the invisible door

understand love
the lesson
the gift
the entry
the wings
the journey.

Australian born **Jade Rosina McCutcheon** holds a Doctor of Creative Arts from the University of Technology, Sydney and a Doctor of Philosophy from the University of Melbourne. She graduated from N.I.D.A. Sydney as a theatre director and has worked in theatre as a professional director and actor trainer for over thirty years. Her publications include books, *Awakening the Performing Body, Embodied Consciousness Performance Technologies, Narrative in Performance,* and chapters in edited, peer reviewed journals and books. Her poetry has been published in Australian poetry journals such as *SCARP, Leaves* and *Wiradjuri* as well as in anthologies, *Terra Incognita*, (Bob Hill publishing 2019, Oregon), */pān| dé| mïk/ 2020: An Anthology of Pandemic Poems, Beyond Words,* and in *The Silent World in her Vase.* Her poem 'Fair Art' won second place in the Kay Snow Awards 2019 and her chapbook *SMALL FEATHER* was published by Finishing Line Press in October 2020. She is a member of the Salem Poetry Project, Artists in Action and the Mid Valley Poetry Society. Her website is: https://www.jaderosinamccutcheon.com/

www.ingramcontent.com/pod-product-compliance
Lightning Source LLC
Chambersburg PA
CBHW022125090426
42743CB00008B/1011